THE JOKE
MUSEUM

D1409651

Robinson Children's Books

THE JOKE
MUSEUM

COMPILED BY SANDY RANSFORD

ILLUSTRATED
BY
DAVID MOSTYN

Robinson Publishing Ltd
7 Kensington Church Court
London W8 4SP

First published in the UK by Robinson Children's Books,
an imprint of Robinson Publishing Ltd, 1996

A copy of the British Library Cataloguing in Publication
Data for this title is available from the British Library.

ISBN 1 85487 479 9

Printed and bound in the EC

10   9   8   7   6   5   4   3   2   1

INTRODUCTION

WELCOME TO THE JOKE MUSEUM, A COLLECTION
OF THE FINEST AND FUNNIEST JOKES IN THE
WORLD! YOU'LL HAVE THE LAUGH OF A LIFETIME
WITH WHAT DINAH SAW, WORKS OF ART, EGYPTIAN
MUMMIES (AND DADDIES), OLD FOSSILS, AND
EVEN OLDER CHESTNUTS. YOU CAN SHIVER IN
THE CHAMBER OF HORRORS, CHUCKLE AT
CENTURIES OF MEDICAL MIRTH WITH OLD
SAWBONES, MARVEL AT SCIENTIFIC GENIUS, SEE
THE WORLD WITH TRAVELLERS' TALES, TAKE
REFRESHMENTS IN YE OLDE MUSEUM TEA
SHOPPE AND SEE IF YOU CAN FIND, HIDDEN
AWAY IN A DARK AND DUSTY CORNER, THE OLDEST
JOKES IN THE WORLD. YOU'VE NEVER SEEN A
MUSEUM LIKE THIS BEFORE, AND YOU'LL NEVER
HAVE SO MUCH FUN IN ONE AGAIN!

SO WHAT ARE YOU WAITING FOR? GO INTO
THE FIRST ROOM AND START LAUGHING!

CONTENTS

INTRODUCTION

ROOM 1

What Dinah Saw....

AN ANCIENT PAPER EATING BUG

WHY COULDN'T THE WOOLLY MAMMOTH TRAVEL ON THE EURO-STAR TRAIN TO PARIS?

BECAUSE HIS TRUNK WOULDN'T FIT IN THE LUGGAGE RACK

What would you give an over-excited Woolly Mammoth?

TRUNKQUILLISERS ZZZZZZZZZZZZ

HOW WOULD YOU STOP A HERD OF WOOLLY MAMMOTHS FROM CHARGING?

TAKE AWAY THEIR CREDIT CARDS

11

TWO FARMERS WERE AT A SALE.
THE FIRST SAID, 'I DON'T KNOW WHETHER TO BUY A COW OR A BICYCLE.'
THE SECOND REPLIED, 'YOU'D LOOK VERY FUNNY RIDING A COW.'
THE FIRST ANSWERED, 'NOT HALF AS FUNNY AS I'D LOOK TRYING TO MILK THE BICYCLE.'

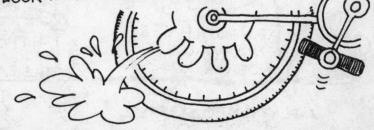

First Cow: Moo.

Second Cow: Baa.

First Cow: What do you mean, baa?

Second Cow: I'm learning a foreign
language.

1947

YEP!

WHERE DO SHEEP DO
THEIR SHOPPING?

1831

WOOLWORTHS

HOLLY: DID YOU
KNOW IT TAKES
THREE SHEEP TO
MAKE ONE
JUMPER?

DOLLY: I DIDN'T
EVEN KNOW SHEEP
COULD KNIT. 1900

HOW DO YOU FEEL IF YOU
SWALLOW A SHEEP?

VERY BAAAAAAD.

WHAT DO YOU GET
IF YOU CROSS A
PORCUPINE WITH
A SHEEP?

AN ANIMAL THAT
KNITS ITS OWN
JUMPERS!

SHEEP JOKES

HARRY   I'VE JUST BOUGHT A PIG.

LARRY   WHERE ARE YOU GOING TO KEEP IT?

HARRY   UNDER MY BED.

LARRY   BUT WHAT ABOUT THE SMELL?

HARRY   OH, THE PIG WON'T MIND THAT.

WHAT DID ONE PIG SAY TO THE OTHER?
'LET'S BE PEN-PALS.'

WHAT'S IT CALLED WHEN PIGS DO THEIR LAUNDRY?
HOGWASH.

HOW DO MONKEYS MAKE TOAST?
PUT BREAD UNDER THE G'RILL-A.

WHAT DO YOU GET IF YOU CROSS A MONKEY WITH A FLOWER?
A CHIMP-PANSY.

WHY DO LIONS EAT RAW MEAT?
THEY'VE NEVER LEARNT TO COOK.

WHAT DO YOU GET IF YOU CROSS A GORILLA WITH A FOOTBALL PLAYER?
———
I DON'T KNOW, BUT IF IT TRIES TO SCORE A GOAL NO ONE TRIES TO STOP IT!

WHY SHOULD YOU NEVER GRAB A LEOPARD BY ITS TAIL?
IT MAY BE ONLY THE LEOPARD'S TAIL BUT IT COULD BE THE END OF YOU.

WHY WAS THE MOTHER TIGER CROSS WHEN SHE FOUND HER CUBS CHASING A TOURIST ROUND A TREE?
BECAUSE SHE'D TOLD THEM NEVER TO PLAY WITH THEIR FOOD.

WHAT GOES 'TICK-TOCK, WOOF'?

A WATCHDOG.

WHAT KIND OF DOGS DO HAIRDRESSERS BREED?

SHAMPOODLES.

JOKES MISSING OWING TO RENOVATION

22

WHAT DO YOU GET IF YOU CROSS A
TERRIER WITH A VEGETABLE?

A JACK BRUSSEL.

WHAT DO CATS EAT FOR BREAKFAST?

MICE KRISPIES

WHY DID THE CAT JOIN THE ST. JOHN'S AMBULANCE BRIGADE?

BECAUSE IT WANTED TO BE A FIRST AID KIT.

ST-AID KIT

24

25

MARY HAD A LITTLE CAT,
SHE ALSO HAD A BEAR.
I'VE OFTEN SEEN HER LITTLE CAT—
BUT I'VE NEVER SEEN HER BARE!
ANON.

I'LL GRAB HER WHEN THE OLD GEEZER TURNS HIS BACK

WHAT'S WHITE, FURRY AND SMELLS OF PEPPERMINTS?

IT MOVED!

A POLO BEAR!

EH?

WHAT DO YOU CALL A BALD KOALA?

FRED BEAR

WHY CAN'T HORSES DANCE?

BECAUSE THEY'VE GOT TWO LEFT FEET.

27

29

WHY IS A BLACK HEN SMARTER THAN A WHITE HEN?

BECAUSE A BLACK HEN CAN LAY WHITE EGGS BUT A WHITE HEN CAN'T LAY BLACK EGGS.

HOW DO BEES KEEP THEIR HAIR TIDY?
WITH HONEYCOMBS.

What's the difference between a
fish and a piano?
YOU CAN'T TUNA FISH.

WHAT'S A FROG'S FAVOURITE DRINK?
CROAKA COLA.

WHAT'S A FROG'S FAVOURITE SWEET?
A LOLLIHOP.

33

ROOM 2

Works of Art...

by painters and sculptors and musicians and writers...

...AND

ME !!!

WHAT COLOURS WOULD YOU PAINT THE
SUN AND THE WIND ?

THE SUN ROSE AND THE WIND BLUE.

36

37

18ᵀᴴ CENTURY ROOM

WHAT HAS EIGHT FEET AND SINGS?
A QUARTET.

WHAT DO YOU CALL A MUSICAL INSECT?
A HUMBUG.

MOTHER: OUR WILFRED LEARNED TO PLAY
THE PIANO IN NO TIME AT ALL.

YES, I HEARD HIM PLAYING
LIKE THAT WHEN I CAME IN.

DARREN   I'VE BORROWED OUR NEIGHBOUR'S
BAGPIPES.

SHARON   BUT YOU CAN'T PLAY THEM.

DARREN   NO, BUT NEITHER CAN HE WHILE
I'VE GOT THEM.

CLARENCE! IT'S TIME FOR YOUR VIOLIN LESSON.

OH, FIDDLE!

DEEPEST GLOOM →

WHY DID SILLY SUE STAND ON A CHAIR WHEN SHE WAS SINGING?

SO SHE COULD REACH THE HIGH NOTES.

WHY DOES THAT STATUE OF THE DUKE OF WELLINGTON STAND IN THE TOWN SQUARE?

BECAUSE HE CAN'T SIT DOWN.

HOW I WON THE LOTTERY
by Jack Pott

HOW I CROSSED THE SAHARA
By Rhoda Camel

EXPLORING AT THE SOUTH POLE
by Anne Tarctic

FALLING DOWN THE CLIFF
by Eileen Dover

VEGETABLE GARDENING
by Rosa Carrots

A POLICEMAN'S JOB
by Laura Norder

ON THE BEACH
by C. Shaw

MATHEMATICS
by Algy Brar

BREAKING WINDOWS
by Eva Brick

SUMMER TREAT
by I. Scream

HOW TO MAKE MONEY
by Robin Banks

GREAT DETECTIVE STORIES
by Hugh Dunnit

SCHOOL DINNERS
by R. Revolting

GIVING PARTIES
by Maud D. Merrier

NOISES IN THE NIGHT
by Constance Norah

MY ACHING JOINTS
by Arthur Ritis

QUICK BREAKFAST
by Roland Butter

INSURING YOUR HOUSE
by Justin Case

MAKING BOMBS
by Dinah Mite

THE OPTIMIST
by Tamara Theworld

KEEP TRYING
by Percy Vere

WEARING WIGS
by Aaron Topp

CAN HE WIN?
by Betty Carnt

CREEPY GHOST STORIES
by R.U. Scared

1ST PASSENGER ON TRAIN	EXCUSE ME, DO YOU KNOW YOU'RE READING YOUR BOOK UPSIDE DOWN?
2ND PASSENGER ON TRAIN	OF COURSE I DO. DO YOU THINK IT'S EASY?

MY SON'S BECOME A WRITER

DOES HE WRITE FOR MONEY?

YES, WITH ALMOST EVERY LETTER HE SENDS.

SHOULD YOU WRITE ON AN EMPTY STOMACH?

YOU COULD, BUT YOU USUALLY USE A DESK.

DAD, CAN YOU WRITE IN THE DARK?

I EXPECT SO. WHY?

WILL YOU SIGN MY REPORT CARD, PLEASE?

45

WHEN YOUNG JENNY WENT TO SCHOOL SHE SAID SHE COULD WRITE BUT NOT READ.
'WRITE YOUR NAME FOR ME THEN,' SAID HER TEACHER.
JENNY SCRIBBLED ON A PIECE OF PAPER AND GAVE IT TO HER TEACHER.
'WHAT DOES THIS SAY?' SHE ASKED.
'I DON'T KNOW,' SAID JENNY, 'I CAN'T READ.'

WHO WROTE 'HOW TO WIN THE NATIONAL LOTTERY'?

IVOR FORTUNE

WHAT HAPPENS IF YOU READ A FIRST-AID BOOK?

WHAT DOES A MUSICIAN NEED IN A SUPERMARKET?

YOU MEET A CHAPTER OF ACCIDENTS.

A CHOPIN LISZT.

WHO SINGS IN LARGE HOTELS?

HILTON JOHN.

47

49

50

LITTLE LUCY WENT TO SEE HER FIRST OPERA.
HER MOTHER ASKED HER HOW SHE'D
LIKED IT.
'I DIDN'T LIKE THAT MAN HITTING THE
LADY WITH HIS STICK,' SHE SAID.
'HE WASN'T HITTING HER, HE WAS
CONDUCTING THE ORCHESTRA,' SAID HER
MOTHER.
'THEN IF HE WASN'T HITTING HER, WHY
WAS SHE SCREAMING?' ASKED LUCY.

DO YOU LIKE OPERA?

APART FROM THE SINGING, YES.

DID YOU HEAR ABOUT THE SILLY MAN
WHO BOUGHT A PIANO STOOL?

HE TOOK IT BACK TO THE SHOP BECAUSE
IT DIDN'T PLAY A NOTE.

52

53

ROOM 3

Egyptian Mummies...

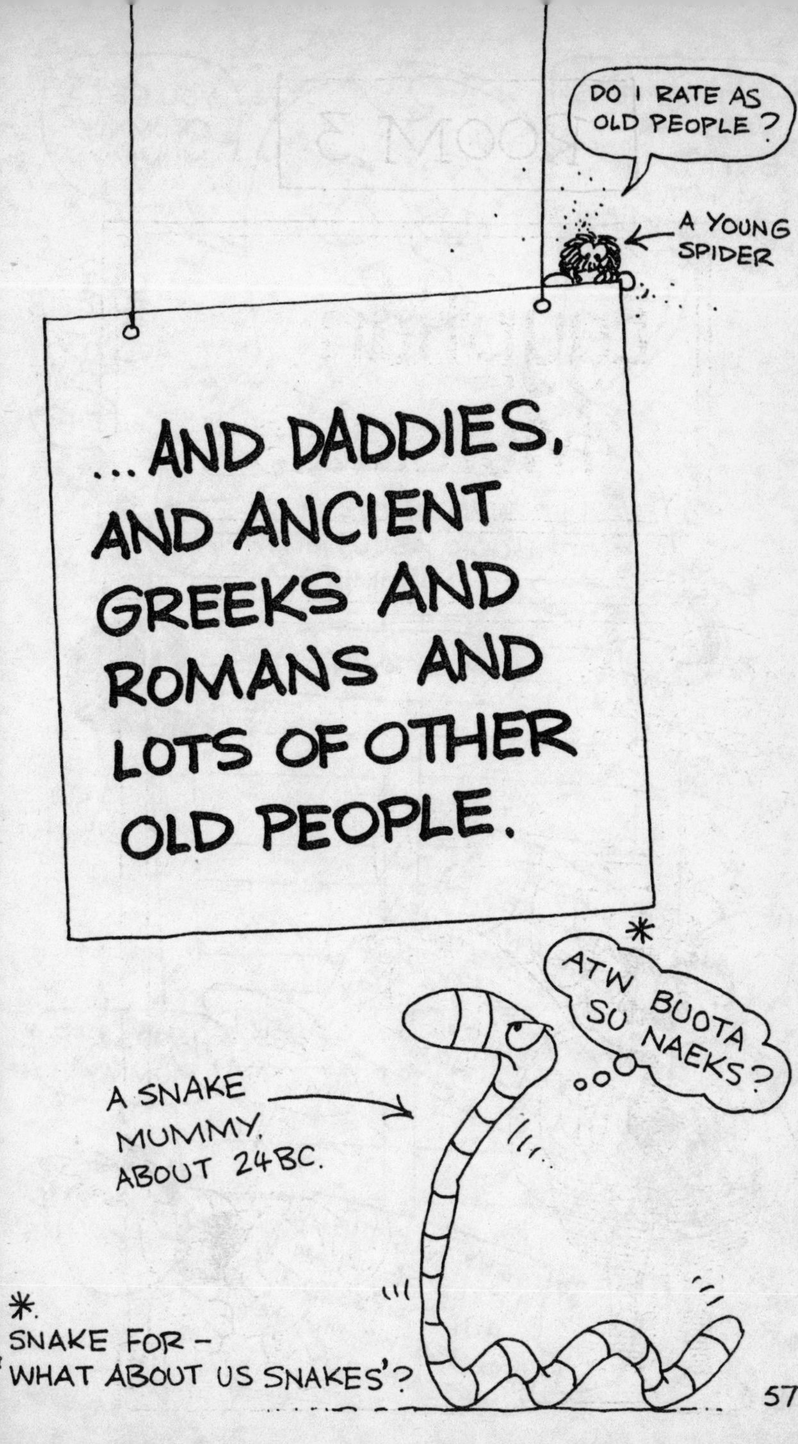
...AND DADDIES, AND ANCIENT GREEKS AND ROMANS AND LOTS OF OTHER OLD PEOPLE.
DO I RATE AS OLD PEOPLE ?
A YOUNG SPIDER
* ATW BUOTA SU NAEKS?
A SNAKE MUMMY, ABOUT 24BC.
*. SNAKE FOR - 'WHAT ABOUT US SNAKES'?

58

A YOUNG EGYPTIAN
GIRL WAS GETTING READY
FOR HER FIRST DISCO, WITH
THE HELP OF HER MOTHER.
'DID YOU GO TO DISCOS WHEN
YOU WERE ALIVE,
MUMMY?'
SHE ASKED.

WHAT DID ONE EGYPTIAN SAY TO ANOTHER?
'I CAN'T REMEMBER YOUR NAME, BUT YOUR FEZ
IS FAMILIAR.' 👁 WHAT DID POLITE ANCIENT
EGYPTIAN CHILDREN CALL THEIR PARENTS?
DEAD AND MUMMY. 👁 LATIN IS A LANGUAGE
DEAD AS DEAD CAN BE. FIRST IT KILLED THE
ROMANS, AND NOW IT'S KILLING ME. 👁
FIRST ROMAN SOLDIER: 'WHAT'S THE TIME?'
SECOND ROMAN SOLDIER: 'XX PAST VI'. 👁
WHY DID ROMANS BUILD STRAIGHT ROADS?
SO THE ANCIENT BRITONS COULDN'T HIDE
ROUND THE CORNERS. 👁 HISTORY TEACHER:
'WHEN WAS ROME BUILT?' CLEVER CLARA:
'AT NIGHT, MISS.' HISTORY TEACHER: 'WHY DO
YOU SAY THAT?' CLEVER CLARA: 'BECAUSE
MUM'S ALWAYS TELLING ME THAT ROME
WASN'T BUILT IN A DAY.' 👁 WHEN A NERVOUS
YOUNG GLADIATOR WAS SENT TO THE CIRCUS
TO FIGHT A LION, HE FAINTED WITH FRIGHT.
WHEN HE RECOVERED, HE SAW THAT THE
LION WAS PRAYING, SO HE SAID, 'THANK YOU
FOR NOT EATING ME.' 'SHH,' SAID THE LION,

'I'M SAYING GRACE.' 👁 TEACHER: 'WHAT WAS THE ROMANS' GREATEST ACHIEVEMENT?' TIM: 'LEARNING LATIN.' 👁 WHY IS A ROOM IN A MUSEUM LIKE A DIRTY OLD FRYING-PAN? BECAUSE IT'S FULL OF ANCIENT GREECE. 👁 TEACHER: 'WHAT'S A GRECIAN URN?' SILLY BILLY: 'ABOUT 50 DRACHMAS A WEEK.' 👁 WHY IS ANCIENT HISTORY LIKE A FRUIT CAKE? BECAUSE IT'S FULL OF DATES. 👁 WHY ARE THE DARK AGES SO CALLED? BECAUSE THEY CONTAINED SO MANY KNIGHTS. 👁 SALLY: 'MY TEACHER WAS CROSS WITH ME BECAUSE I DIDN'T KNOW WHERE THE PYRAMIDS WERE.' SALLY'S MUM: 'I'M ALWAYS TELLING YOU TO REMEMBER WHERE YOU'VE PUT THINGS.' 👁 TEACHER: 'WHO INVENTED THE ROUND TABLE?' DAFT DAVE: 'SIR CUMFERENCE, MISS.' 👁 WHAT WAS KING ARTHUR'S FAVOURITE GAME? KNIGHTS AND CROSSES. 👁 WHICH KNIGHT NEVER WON A BATTLE? SIR RENDER. 👁 WHICH ENGLISH KING BURNT THE CAKES? ALFRED THE GRATE.

62

ON LOAN FROM PAGE 153

63

65

WHERE DID NOAH KEEP HIS BEES?
IN THE ARK HIVES.

WHAT WAS CAMELOT
FAMOUS FOR?
IT'S KNIGHT LIFE.

TEA ROOMS   TOILET

WHY DID ELIZABETH I WEAR LONG
WOOLLY BLOOMERS?
TO KEEP WARM, OF COURSE!

WHAT WAS THE FIRST THING
HENRY VI DID ON COMING TO THE
THRONE? SAT DOWN.

SOUVENIR SHOP   EXIT

THERE'S NOTHING FOR US DOGS.

KNOCK, KNOCK.
WHO'S THERE?
HOMER.
HOMER WHO?
HOMER AGAIN.

WHO WAS IVANHOE?
A RUSSIAN GARDENER.

IN WHICH BATTLE WAS NELSON
KILLED? HIS LAST ONE.

TEACHER: CAN YOU TELL ME
WHAT NATIONALITY NAPOLEON
WAS, NIGEL?
RONALD: CORSICAN!

TEACHER: WHAT CAN YOU TELL ME ABOUT
JOAN OF ARC?

DOPEY: SHE WAS MADE IN ORLÉANS.

HOW DID THE VIKINGS SEND SECRET MESSAGES?
BY NORSE CODE.

TEACHER

DOES ANYONE KNOW WHEN QUEEN ELIZABETH II'S BIRTHDAY IS ?

HARRY

ON 21ST APRIL, MISS.

TEACHER

WHICH YEAR ?

HARRY

EVERY YEAR.

A CLASS OF SCHOOLCHILDREN WAS BEING TAUGHT ABOUT JESUS AND HIS DISCIPLES.

'CAN YOU TELL ME WHO PETER WAS ?' ASKED THE TEACHER.

A SMALL GIRL PUT UP HER HAND.

'PLEASE, MISS,' SHE SAID, 'HE WAS A RABBIT.'

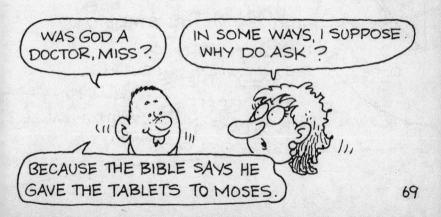

WAS GOD A DOCTOR, MISS ?

IN SOME WAYS, I SUPPOSE. WHY DO ASK ?

BECAUSE THE BIBLE SAYS HE GAVE THE TABLETS TO MOSES.

CATALOGUE

WHAT DID ONE ANGEL SAY TO
ANOTHER ?
'HALO !'

WHO LOST AT WATERLOO AND EXPLODED ?
NAPOLEON BLOWNAPART.

HOW DO WE KNOW THAT MOSES
WORE A WIG ?
BECAUSE SOMETIMES HE WAS SEEN
WITH AARON AND SOMETIMES WITHOUT.

WHO WAS THE FIRST CHIROPODIST ?
WILLIAM THE CORNCURER.

MOLLY I WISH I'D BEEN
BORN IN THE STONE AGE.
POLLY WHY ?
MOLLY THERE WOULDN'T
HAVE BEEN SO MUCH
HISTORY TO LEARN.

WHERE DID KING JOHN
KEEP HIS ARMIES ?

UP HIS SLEEVIES.

YOU CAN SEE THIS JOKE IN ROOM 14
ON THURSDAY AND SATURDAY.
ON LOAN BY KIND PERMISSION
OF ROLAND MILK OF PECKHAM.

WHAT DID LOT DO WITH HIS WIFE AFTER SHE'D BEEN TURNED INTO A PILLAR OF SALT?

PUT HER IN THE CELLAR.

TEACHER: Can you name the Tudor monarchs?

MAGGIE: Henry VII, Henry VIII, Edward VI, Mary, er...

TEACHER: Who came after Mary?

MAGGIE: The little lamb?

Where did most sword fights take place?

On duel carriageways.

DO NOT TOUCH
DO NOT COUGH
DO NOT LOOK

DO NOT DO NOTHING!!

THE POOR DIDN'T HAVE ANYTHING WORTH STEALING!

QUIET PLEASE

IT'S SUSPICIOUSLY QUIET

WHO LED AN ARMY OF CONVENT GIRLS?

ATTILA THE NUN

WHO WAS MEXICO'S MOST
FAMOUS FAT MAN ? PAUNCHO VILLA.

WHERE WERE ENGLISH
KINGS CROWNED?
ON THE HEAD.

NOT
THERE

ANCIENT MUM.
C.1932

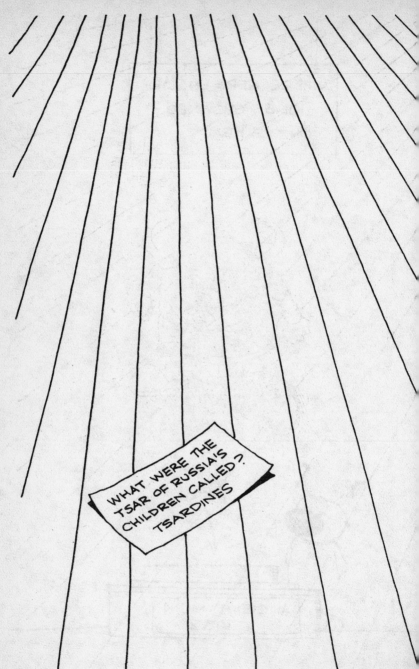

HOW DID HIAWATHA ?
WITH THOAP AND HOT WATER .

TEACHER: WHO CAN TELL ME WHERE
HADRIAN'S WALL IS ?

SILLY SIDNEY : ROUND HADRIAN'S
GARDEN.

LEN: DAVY CROCKETT HAD THREE EARS.

BEN: HE COULDN'T HAVE !

LEN: HE DID. HE HAD A RIGHT EAR,
A LEFT EAR AND A WILD
FRONTIER.

WHO INVENTED THE FIVE-DAY WEEK ?
ROBINSON CRUSOE- HE HAD ALL HIS
WORK DONE BY FRIDAY.

COR! HEAVY JOKES!

WHAT CAKE WANTED TO RULE THE WORLD?
ATTILA THE BUN.

WHO RODE A CAMEL AND CARRIED A LAMP?

WHO WAS THE BLACK PRINCE? OLD KING COLE'S SON.

FLORENCE OF ARABIA.

HETTIE: I'VE BEEN LEARNING ANCIENT HISTORY.

BETTY: SO HAVE I! LET'S GO FOR A WALK AND TALK ABOUT OLD TIMES.

ENGLISH GIRL: My great-great grandfather was touched on the shoulder with a sword by King Edward VII, and that made him a knight.

AMERICAN GIRL: So what? One of my ancestors was touched on the head with a tomahawk by a Cheyenne Indian and that made him an angel.

GOOD, EH!

ROOM 4

Old Fossils...

...some very good old jokes in here!

BOSS: WHY DO YOU WANT NEXT WEEK OFF?

CLERK: I'M GETTING MARRIED, SIR.

BOSS: WHAT KIND OF IDIOT GIRL WOULD MARRY YOU?

CLERK: YOUR DAUGHTER, SIR.

CLERK: MAY I HAVE AN HOUR OFF TO HAVE MY HAIR CUT?

BOSS: CERTAINLY NOT. HAVE IT CUT IN YOUR OWN TIME.

CLERK: BUT IT GROWS IN OFFICE HOURS.

BOSS: IT DOESN'T DO ALL ITS GROWING IN OFFICE HOURS, THOUGH.

CLERK: NO, BUT I'M NOT HAVING IT ALL CUT OFF!

ANGRY NEIGHBOUR:

COME HERE! I'LL TEACH YOU TO THROW STONES AT MY GREENHOUSE!

NAUGHTY NIGEL:

I ALREADY KNOW HOW.

I LIKE IT!

ANNIE

What are you going to give your baby sister
for Christmas?

DANNY

Well, last Christmas I gave her measles...

83

ADAM WAS NAMING THE ANIMALS.

'THIS,' HE SAID, 'IS A HIPPOPOTAMUS.'

'WHY IS IT?' ASKED EVE.

'BECAUSE IT LOOKS LIKE A HIPPOPOTAMUS, SILLY!'

85

SAY THIS TO A FRIEND:

ADAM AND EVE AND PINCH ME
WENT DOWN TO THE SEA TO BATHE.
ADAM AND EVE BOTH GOT DROWNED,
WHO D'YOU THINK WAS SAVED?

AND WHEN YOUR FRIEND ANSWERS, 'PINCH ME'...!

EVIL TITTER

YEOW!

OW!

AAAH!

OUCH!

OOOH!!

OUCH!

YEOWCH!

TWO GIRLS WERE DISCUSSING THEIR NOT VERY
BRIGHT FRIEND. 'I WOULDN'T SAY SHE WAS
STUPID,' SAID THE FIRST, 'BUT WHEN SHE WENT
TO A MIND-READER HE GAVE HER HER
MONEY BACK.'

WHAT CAN YOU HAVE
IN AN EMPTY POCKET?

A HOLE!

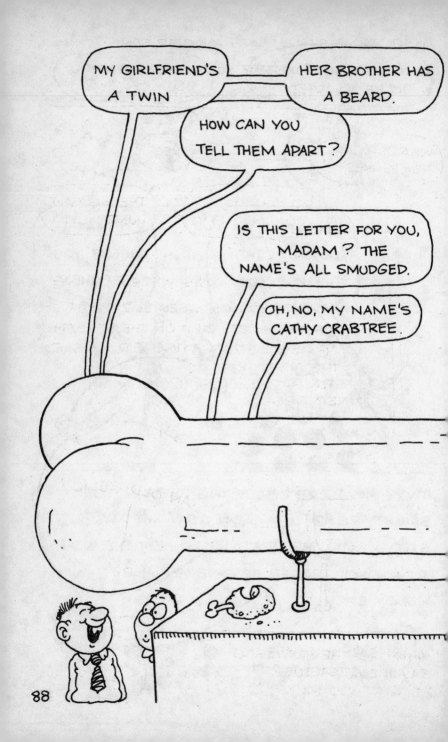

LITTLE LUCY: SHALL I SING ANOTHER SONG?

AUNTIE SARAH: NO, DEAR, YOU'VE DELIGHTED

US LONG ENOUGH.

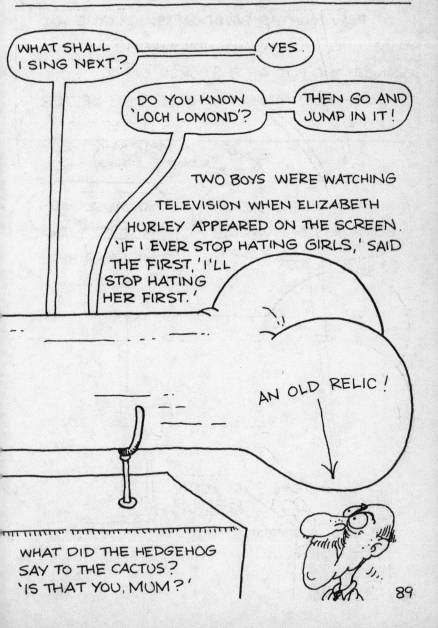

WHAT SHALL I SING NEXT?

YES.

DO YOU KNOW 'LOCH LOMOND'?

THEN GO AND JUMP IN IT!

TWO BOYS WERE WATCHING TELEVISION WHEN ELIZABETH HURLEY APPEARED ON THE SCREEN. 'IF I EVER STOP HATING GIRLS,' SAID THE FIRST, 'I'LL STOP HATING HER FIRST.'

AN OLD RELIC!

WHAT DID THE HEDGEHOG SAY TO THE CACTUS? 'IS THAT YOU, MUM?'

89

CHARLIE WAS LEARNING TO DRIVE. HIS BROTHER
ANDY ASKED HIM WHAT THE L STOOD FOR ON THE
L PLATE. 'LEARNER,' SAID CHARLIE.

A FEW MONTHS LATER, AFTER CHARLIE HAD
PASSED HIS TEST HE WAS TAKING HIS CAR TO
FRANCE AND PUT A GB STICKER ON IT.

'DOES THAT MEAN YOU'RE GETTING BETTER?'
ASKED ANDY.

MY SISTER'S JUST GOT ENGAGED TO
AN IRISHMAN.

OH, REALLY?   NO, O'REILLY.

SAMMY: TELEVISION WILL NEVER REPLACE NEWSPAPERS.

TAMMY: Why do you say that?

SAMMY: HAVE YOU EVER TRIED WRAPPING YOUR FISH AND CHIPS IN A TELEVISION?

EH?

IS THAT AN OLD FOSSIL?

CAN YOU SPELL 'BANANA'?

WELL, I CAN START, BUT I'M NOT SURE WHEN TO STOP.

BANANANA
NANANAN
ANANAN
ANANAN
ANANAN

SHOPPER: A MOUSETRAP, PLEASE, AND BE QUICK, I'VE GOT A TRAIN TO CATCH! SHOP ASSISTANT: I HAVEN'T ANYTHING THAT BIG, MADAM.

93

WHY DID THE CAR GET A PUNCTURE?

THERE WAS A FORK IN THE ROAD

"EVIL GLINTER!!!"

HISS!!

TRAVELLER: HOW MUCH TO TAKE ME TO THE STATION?

TAXI-DRIVER: FIVE POUNDS, SIR.

TRAVELLER: AND HOW MUCH FOR MY SUITCASE?

TAXI-DRIVER: OH, I WOULDN'T CHARGE FOR THAT, SIR.

TRAVELLER: OK, YOU TAKE THE CASE AND I'LL WALK.

CUTHBERT! WHY DID YOU PUT A WORM IN YOUR SISTER'S BED?

I COULDN'T FIND A TOAD.

SCREAM!!
SOB!!

TEACHER: HAVE YOU READ YOUR

HISTORY TEXTBOOK, EVANS?

EVANS: NO, SIR.

TEACHER: AND HAVE YOU READ YOUR

SHAKESPEARE OR YOUR DICKENS?

EVANS: NO, SIR.

TEACHER: WELL, HAVE YOU READ ANYTHING?

EVANS: I'VE RED HAIR, SIR.

BARBER: AND HOW WOULD YOU LIKE YOUR
HAIR CUT, YOUNG MAN?

ERIC: LIKE DAD'S, WITH A HOLE IN THE TOP.

WHO WAS THAT AT THE DOOR?

A man with a wooden leg.

TELL HIM TO HOP IT.

DID YOU HEAR ABOUT THE MAN WHO SENT
HIS PHOTOGRAPH TO THE LONELY HEARTS CLUB?
THEY WROTE BACK SAYING THEY WEREN'T
THAT LONELY.

C.1901

BEN: I've lost my dog.

I CAN!

KEN: Why don't you put an advertisement in the local paper?

BEN: Don't be silly, he can't read.

GENUINE OLD POLICE JOKES

DID YOU HEAR THAT THE POLICE ARE LOOKING FOR A MAN WITH A WOODEN LEG?

WHY DON'T THEY USE SPECTACLES?

GENUINE OLD POLICEMAN

A POLICEMAN WAS TAKING A CRIMINAL TO PRISON WHEN HIS HAT BLEW OFF.

'SHALL I GO AND GET IT FOR YOU?' ASKED THE CRIMINAL.

'YOU MUST THINK I'M STUPID,' SAID THE POLICEMAN. 'YOU STAY HERE AND I'LL GET IT.' 97

TEACHER: WHY ARE YOU
             LATE FOR SCHOOL?

MIKE: I BRUISED SOME FINGERS KNOCKING A
            NAIL IN THE WALL AT HOME.

TEACHER: YOUR FINGERS LOOK ALL RIGHT TO ME.

MIKE: THEY WEREN'T MY FINGERS!

MAVE: I'LL RECITE A POEM.

'THERE ONCE WAS A LADY NAMED NELLIE,

WHO WADED IN THE SEA UP TO HER KNEES...'

DAVE: IT DOESN'T RHYME.

MAVE: NO. THE WATER WAS TOO COLD FOR HER

TO GO IN ANY DEEPER.

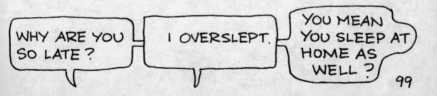

WHAT GOES IN PINK
AND COMES OUT BLUE?

A SWIMMER ON
A COLD DAY.

Sign in a travel
agent's window:

PLEASE GO AWAY.

WHICH WAY?

SIGN AT A RAILWAY STATION:

WE REGRET THESE TOILETS ARE CLOSED.
PLEASE USE PLATFORM 5.

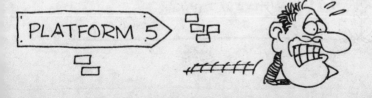

PLATFORM 5

SIGN IN A FURNITURE STORE :

FOAM CUSHIONS.
ROCK BOTTOM PRICES.

FOR SALE : DELICATE VICTORIAN CHINA VASE, THE
PROPERTY OF AN ELDERLY LADY,
ONLY SLIGHTLY CRACKED.

FOR SALE:

THATCHED COUNTRY COTTAGE, TWO
BEDROOMS, LARGE LIVING-ROOM,
MODERN BATHROOM, SEPARATE
TOILET TEN MILES FROM
SOUTHAMPTON.

FOR SALE: 1935 ROLLS ROYCE HEARSE.
ORIGINAL BODY.

THAT'S ABOUT ME, THAT IS!

FOR SALE: ALSATIAN PUPPY. HOUSE-TRAINED, GENTLE, WILL EAT ANYTHING, ESPECIALLY FOND OF CHILDREN.

EXTRA PLUMP
KIDS

SALLY: Mm! This cake's all lovely and warm!

GULP!!

WALLY: It should be, the cat's been sitting on it all day.

YEAH! GREAT CAKE!!

103

MUM: THERE WERE TWO TRIFLES IN THE FRIDGE YESTERDAY AND NOW THERE'S ONLY ONE. WHY?

SAMMY: THE SECOND ONE MUST HAVE BEEN HIDDEN BEHIND SOMETHING ELSE.

TEACHER: CAN YOU QUOTE ANYTHING FROM THE
BIBLE?

MARY: 'JUDAS DEPARTED, AND WENT AND
HANGED HIMSELF.'

TEACHER: VERY GOOD. ANYTHING ELSE?

MARY: 'GO THOU AND DO LIKEWISE.'

TEACHER: YOU WEREN'T AT SCHOOL YESTERDAY,
PETER. I HEARD YOU WERE OUT PLAYING
FOOTBALL INSTEAD.

PETER: THAT'S NOT TRUE, SIR, AND I'VE GOT
A FISH TO PROVE IT.

105

HOW DOES A MONSTER COUNT TO 13?

ON ITS FINGERS.

WHAT DO MONSTERS HAVE
AT 11 O'CLOCK EACH MORNING?

A COFFIN BREAK.

113

114

WHY ARE GRAVEYARDS SO NOISY?
BECAUSE OF THE COFFIN.

HOW DO YOU TELL IF SOMEONE HAS A GLASS EYE?

WHEN IT COMES OUT IN CONVERSATION.

A RARE EXAMPLE OF NAUGHTY 17TH CENTURY GRAFFITI!

A RARE EXAMPLE OF 20TH CENTURY GRAFFITI

HOW DID KING HENRY STOP HIS SON FROM BITING HIS NAILS?

HE CUT ALL HIS FINGERS OFF.

FIRST CANNIBAL: I DON'T KNOW WHAT TO MAKE OF MY HUSBAND NOWADAYS.

SECOND CANNIBAL: HOW ABOUT A HOTPOT?

WHAT DOES A HEADLESS HORSEMAN RIDE?

A NIGHTMARE.

FRSXX!!

WHAT DID THE MONSTERS LIKE TO WATCH ON TELEVISION?

HORROR-NATION STREET.

* HORSE FOR 'GULP!'

WHAT IS A SEA MONSTER'S FAVOURITE FOOD?

FISH AND SHIPS.

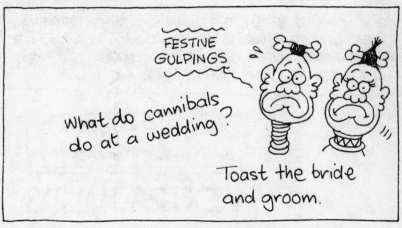

FESTIVE GULPINGS

What do cannibals do at a wedding?

Toast the bride and groom.

HOW CAN YOU HELP A STARVING CANNIBAL?

Give him a hand.

WHAT HAPPENED WHEN THE CANNIBALS ATE THE COMEDIAN?

THEY HAD A FEAST OF FUN.

DID YOU HEAR ABOUT THE CANNIBAL WHO WENT ON A SEA VOYAGE? WHEN HE SAT DOWN FOR DINNER ON THE FIRST NIGHT OUT HE SENT BACK THE MENU AND ASKED FOR THE PASSENGER LIST.

ANTIQUE SIGN FROM A BACON-SLICING FACTORY:

EXTRA HANDS NEEDED.

TWO LITTLE GIRLS WERE PADDLING AT THE
SEASIDE. 'COO!' SAID ONE, 'AREN'T YOUR FEET
DIRTY!'

'THEY ARE A BIT,' REPLIED THE OTHER, 'BUT,
YOU SEE, WE DIDN'T COME LAST YEAR.'

121

A LITTLE BOY AT SCOUT CAMP
WAS BEING TOLD OFF FOR
BEING LATE BACK.
'WHY ARE YOU SO LATE?'
ASKED THE SCOUTMASTER.
'WELL,' SAID THE LITTLE BOY,
'WHEN WE CROSSED THAT
FIELD OF COWS MY BERET
BLEW OFF AND I HAD TO
TRY ON 20 BEFORE I
FOUND IT.'

WHAT'S BROWN
AND COMES STEAMING
OUT OF COWES?

THE ISLE OF
WIGHT FERRY.

123

124

WHAT'S THE DIFFERENCE BETWEEN A RAILWAY
GUARD AND A TEACHER ?
ONE MINDS THE TRAIN, THE OTHER TRAINS
THE MIND.

TRAIN
PASSENGER: DOES THIS TRAIN STOP AT DOVER?

TICKET
COLLECTOR: IF IT DOESN'T THERE'LL BE AN
ALMIGHTY SPLASH!

'MUM, WHAT WAS THAT STATION
WE JUST PASSED THROUGH?'
'I DON'T KNOW, DEAR, I WAS
READING. WHY DO YOU WANT
TO KNOW?
'BECAUSE IT'S WHERE MY
SISTER FELL OUT.'

WHY DO TRAFFIC LIGHTS
TURN RED ?

YOU'D TURN RED IF YOU HAD
TO STOP AND GO IN THE MIDDLE
OF THE STREET !

GRANDMA FELL DOWN THE STEPS LAST WEEK.

NO, WE THINK SHE CAN BE REPAIRED.

CELLAR ?

FIRST CANNIBAL: I DON'T LIKE MY NEIGHBOUR.

SECOND CANNIBAL: I DON'T LIKE HIM MUCH EITHER. LET'S ADD A BIT MORE SALT AND PEPPER.

127

129

130

WHY DIDN'T THE SKELETON GO TO THE DISCO?

BECAUSE HE HAD NOBODY TO DANCE WITH.

THAT'S RIGHT!

FIRST WITCH: A BLACK CAT JUST WALKED IN.

SECOND WITCH: BLACK CATS ARE LUCKY.

FIRST WITCH: THIS ONE WASN'T. IT ATE OUR DINNER.

CHEEK!

What do you say to a witch after you've told her a joke?

Cut the cackle.

131

MR COLLIEWOBBLE:

Hello, dear. I've brought a friend home for dinner.

MRS. COLLIEWOBBLE:

You might have warned me. I've spent all day preparing a stew.

WHAT HAPPENS WHEN TWO SNAILS HAVE A FIGHT?

THEY SLUG IT OUT.

WHO WROTE DROOPY DRAWERS?

LUCY LASTIC.

133

NERVOUS PASSENGER: HOW FAR ARE WE FROM LAND?

SHIP'S CAPTAIN: ABOUT TWO MILES.

NERVOUS PASSENGER: IS THAT ALL? IN WHICH DIRECTION?

SHIP'S CAPTAIN: DOWNWARDS.

LILY: MUMMY, MUMMY, BILLY'S BROKEN MY DOLL!

MOTHER: HOW DID HE DO THAT?

LILY: I HIT HIM OVER THE HEAD WITH IT.

TOURIST IN PARIS: WE'VE BEEN HERE A WEEK AND WE HAVEN'T BEEN TO THE LOUVRE YET.

SECOND TOURIST IN PARIS: I KNOW, IT MUST BE THE WATER.

DO YOU KNOW ANYONE WHO'S BEEN ON THE TELLY?

MY LITTLE BROTHER DID ONCE, BUT HE USES THE TOILET NOW.

ON A FLIGHT FROM LONDON TO AUSTRALIA A NAUGHTY CHILD WAS GETTING ON THE PASSENGERS' NERVES. ONE MAN COULD STAND IT NO LONGER. 'HEY, SONNY,' HE SAID, 'WHY DON'T YOU GO AND PLAY OUTSIDE?'

PENNY: WHO'S THAT LARGE LADY WITH THE RED HAIR AND THE LITTLE WART?

LENNY: SHH, THAT'S HER HUSBAND.

ROOM 6

Ye Olde Museum Tea Shoppe

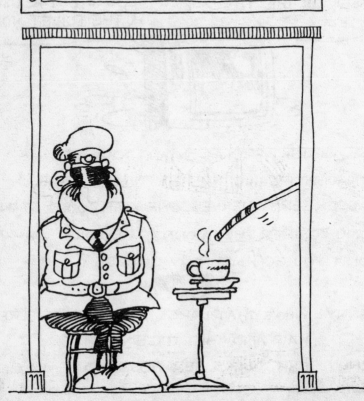

WHAT KIND OF SANDWICH SPEAKS FOR ITSELF?

A TONGUE SANDWICH.

WHAT'S WORSE THAN FINDING A CATERPILLAR IN YOUR SALAD SANDWICH?

FINDING HALF A CATERPILLAR!

NERVOUS GULP!

BILL: Will you join me in a bowl of soup?

BEN: Do you think there's room for both of us?

DINER: WHAT KIND OF SOUP IS THIS?

WAITER: IT'S BEAN SOUP, MADAM.

DINER: I DON'T CARE WHAT IT'S BEEN, WHAT IS IT NOW?

DINER: HOW LONG DO YOU COOK YOUR SPAGHETTI?

WAITER: ABOUT 30 CENTIMETRES, SIR.

WILL MY PIZZA BE LONG?

NO, SIR, ROUND, LIKE EVERYONE ELSE'S.

GURGLING!

CHEESE, HAM, ONIONS, AND EXTRA SALAMI.

139

WHAT HAPPENED TO THAT CAKE YOU MADE ?

I'M AFRAID THE DOG
STOLE IT.

OH DEAR. STILL, I SUPPOSE WE CAN GET
ANOTHER DOG.

141

142

143

145

WAITER, IS THERE FRUIT YOGHURT ON THE MENU?

THERE WAS, SIR, BUT I'VE WIPED IT OFF.

YOU'RE NOT FIT TO SERVE A PIG!

I'M DOING MY BEST, SIR.

NEIGH!

WHY HAVE YOU SERVED MY DINNER IN A NOSEBAG?

I'D HEARD YOU EAT LIKE A HORSE, SIR.

UGH!

DINER: I'LL HAVE SOME BURNT BACON, GREASY SAUSAGES, A HARD FRIED EGG AND COLD CHIPS.

WAITER: WE CAN'T POSSIBLY SERVE YOU FOOD LIKE THAT, SIR.

DINER: WHY NOT? YOU DID YESTERDAY.

DINER: WAITER, I CAN'T EAT THIS FOOD, IT'S DISGUSTING. FETCH ME THE MANAGER.

WAITER: IT'S NO USE, SIR, HE WON'T EAT IT EITHER.

DINER: HOW LONG HAVE YOU WORKED HERE?

WAITER: TWO MONTHS, SIR.

DINER: OH, SO IT CAN'T BE YOU WHO TOOK MY ORDER.

CUSTOMER: I'D LIKE AN ELEPHANT SANDWICH, IN BROWN BREAD, WITH TOMATO KETCHUP, PLEASE.

WAITER: I'M SORRY, MADAM, I CAN'T SERVE YOU WITH THAT.

CUSTOMER: WHY NOT?

WAITER: WE'RE RIGHT OUT OF BROWN BREAD.

CUSTOMER: A CROCODILE ON TOAST, PLEASE, AND MAKE IT SNAPPY!

CUSTOMER: HOW MUCH DO YOU CHARGE FOR DINNER? WAITER: £25 A HEAD, SIR.

CUSTOMER: IN THAT CASE JUST BRING ME A NOSE.

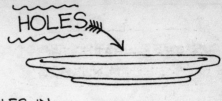

HOLES

MUM, I DON'T LIKE
THIS CHEESE WITH HOLES IN.

DON'T BE SILLY. EAT
THE CHEESE AND LEAVE
THE HOLES ON THE SIDE
OF THE PLATE.

I LIKE HOLES,
I DO!

I EAT MY PEAS WITH HONEY,
I'VE DONE IT ALL MY LIFE.
IT MIGHT SEEM KIND OF FUNNY,
BUT IT KEEPS THEM ON THE KNIFE.

DINER: DO YOU HAVE FROGS' LEGS?
WAITER: YES, SIR.
DINER: THEN HOP ALONG TO THE
KITCHEN AND BRING ME AN
OMELETTE.

149

CUSTOMER: Is this tea or coffee? It tastes like turpentine.

WAITER: Then it's coffee, sir. The tea tastes like petrol.

FIRST DINER: I THINK I'LL HAVE A TONGUE
SANDWICH.

SECOND DINER: UGH! I COULDN'T EAT ANYTHING
THAT HAD COME OUT OF AN
ANIMAL'S MOUTH.

FIRST DINER: WHAT ARE YOU GOING TO HAVE,
THEN?

SECOND DINER: I'LL HAVE SOME EGGS ON TOAST.

WHY IS A HOT DOG THE BEST OF ALL DOGS ?
BECAUSE IT FEEDS THE HAND THAT BITES IT.

WHY ARE SARDINES THE MOST STUPID FISH
IN THE SEA ?
BECAUSE THEY GO INTO TINS, LOCK THEMSELVES
IN AND LEAVE THE KEY ON THE OUTSIDE.

TWO KEEN GARDENERS WERE ENJOYING A CUP
OF TEA IN THE MUSEUM CAFÉ.
'WHAT DO YOU PUT ON YOUR STRAWBERRIES?'
ASKED THE FIRST.
'YOU CAN'T BEAT WELL-ROTTED HORSE MANURE,'
HE ANSWERED.
'REALLY?' REPLIED THE FIRST. 'I LIKE CREAM
ON MINE.'

WHY IS ROAST PORK
LIKE AN OLD RADIO?

THEY BOTH HAVE
A LOT OF
CRACKLING.

DID YOU HEAR ABOUT
THE NEW 'TWO-HANDED'
CHEESE? YOU EAT IT
WITH ONE HAND AND
HOLD YOUR NOSE WITH
THE OTHER.

PORK-LIKE
TWIDDLINGS!!

153

155

HOW DO YOU MAKE A BANANA SPLIT?

CUT IT IN HALF.

WHAT'S YELLOW
AND
DANGEROUS?

SHARK-INFESTED
CUSTARD.

MOTHER: EAT UP YOUR SPINACH, SAMANTHA, IT'LL PUT COLOUR IN YOUR CHEEKS.

SAMANTHA: BUT I DON'T WANT GREEN CHEEKS!

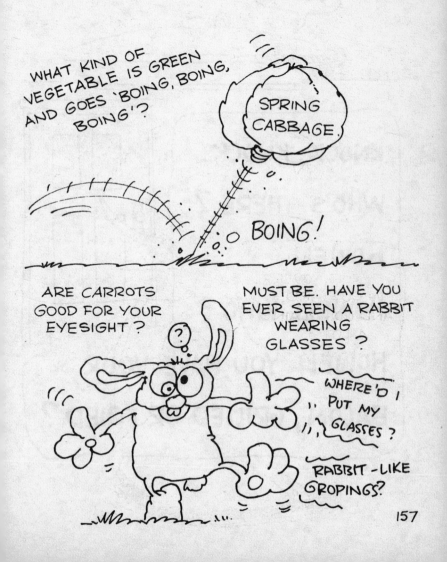

WHAT KIND OF VEGETABLE IS GREEN AND GOES 'BOING, BOING, BOING'?

SPRING CABBAGE

BOING!

ARE CARROTS GOOD FOR YOUR EYESIGHT?

MUST BE. HAVE YOU EVER SEEN A RABBIT WEARING GLASSES?

WHERE'D I PUT MY GLASSES?

RABBIT-LIKE GROPINGS?

THERE'S NO HAM IN THIS VEAL AND HAM PIE.

AND THERE ARE NO SHEPHERDS IN THE SHEPHERDS PIE, EITHER.

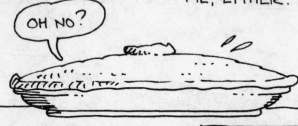

OH NO?

KNOCK, KNOCK.

WHO'S THERE?

HOWELL.

HOWELL WHO?

HOWELL YOU HAVE YOUR BACON, GRILLED OR FRIED?

WHAT DO ATHLETES ORDER IN THE CAFÉ?

RUNNER BEANS.

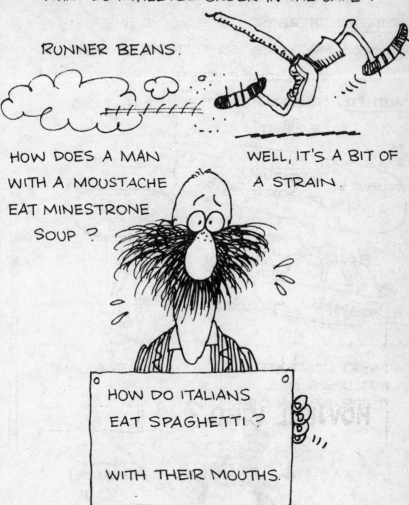

HOW DOES A MAN WITH A MOUSTACHE EAT MINESTRONE SOUP?

WELL, IT'S A BIT OF A STRAIN.

HOW DO ITALIANS EAT SPAGHETTI?

WITH THEIR MOUTHS.

JOHNNY: GULP! I THINK I'VE JUST SWALLOWED A BONE. MUM: ARE YOU CHOKING? JOHNNY: NO, I'M SERIOUS.

DONNY: I THOUGHT YOU SAID WE'D HAVE A CHOICE
OF FOOD FOR LUNCH TODAY.

MOTHER: THERE IS.

DONNY: NO THERE ISN'T. THERE'S JUST
MACARONI CHEESE.

MOTHER: YOU CAN CHOOSE TO EAT IT OR
LEAVE IT.

WHAT DO TRAFFIC
WARDENS LIKE IN
THEIR SANDWICHES?

TRAFFIC JAM.

DINER: WHY ARE YOU BRINGING ME A CRAB
WITH ONLY ONE CLAW?

WAITER: I'M SORRY, SIR, IT MUST HAVE BEEN
IN A FIGHT.

DINER: IN THAT CASE BRING ME THE WINNER.

DINER: WAITER, DO YOU SERVE WILD BOAR?

WAITER: NO, BUT WE CAN TAKE A TAME ONE AND MAKE HIM ANGRY FOR YOU.

SHOULD YOU EAT CHIPS WITH YOUR FINGERS?

NO, FINGERS SHOULD BE EATEN SEPARATELY.

WHAT DO YOU GET IF YOU CROSS A STRAWBERRY WITH AN ELK?

STRAWBERRY MOUSSE.

BETTY: HAVE A SLICE OF THIS CAKE I MADE THIS MORNING.

HETTIE: UGH! IT'S HORRIBLE!

BETTY: NO IT ISN'T. THE RECIPE SAYS QUITE PLAINLY THAT IT'S DELICIOUS.

ROOM 7

Travellers' Tales . . .

... jokes from around the world

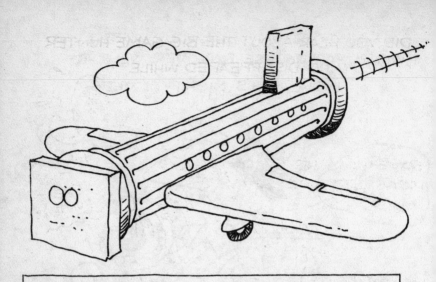

HOW DID THE ANCIENT EGYPTIANS TRAVEL?

BY PHAROAH PLANE.

A CLUMSY YOUNG SAILOR NAMED SCOTT
TRIED CROSSING THE CHANNEL BY YACHT.
WHEN BLOWN OFF HIS COURSE,
HE TAPPED OUT IN MORSE,
'DOT, DOT, DOT; DASH, DASH, DASH;
DOT, DOT, DOT.'

(This is the SOS signal in Morse code.)

DID YOU HEAR ABOUT THE BIG GAME HUNTER
WHO DISAPPEARED WHILE
ON SAFARI ?

SOMETHING HE
DISAGREED WITH
ATE HIM.

YUM!
GREAT
HUNTER!

MRS WIDEHIPS: THEY SAY TRAVEL BROADENS
THE MIND. I'VE TRAVELLED A LOT.
MRS SLIMHIPS: THAT'S NOT ALL IT BROADENS,
THEN.

MR MOUSETROUSER: MY WIFE'S GONE TO THE
WEST INDIES.
MR RATPANTS: JAMAICA?
MR MOUSETROUSER: NO, SHE WENT OF HER OWN
FREE WILL.

A LADY WHO PLANNED TO FLY FROM LONDON TO
NEW YORK RANG THE TRAVEL AGENT TO SEE HOW
LONG THE FLIGHT WOULD BE.
'JUST A MINUTE,' SAID THE GIRL WHO ANSWERED
THE PHONE.
'THANK YOU,' REPLIED THE CALLER, AND HUNG UP.

MR AND MRS DINWIDDIE WERE GOING ON THEIR
FIRST HOLIDAY ABROAD, AND MRS DINWIDDIE
HAD SPENT A LONG TIME FUSSING OVER WHAT
THEY SHOULD TAKE WITH THEM. AT LAST THEY
ARRIVED AT THE AIRPORT.
'I DO WISH I'D BROUGHT THE TELEVISION,'
SIGHED MRS DINWIDDIE.
'WHATEVER FOR?' ASKED HER HUSBAND.
'I LEFT THE TICKETS ON IT,' REPLIED HIS WIFE.

WHY CAN'T A
CAR PLAY FOOTBALL?

IT'S ONLY GOT
ONE BOOT.

171

CARRIE: HOW MANY MEALS DID THEY SERVE
ON YOUR SAIL ROUND THE ISLANDS?

LARRY: FOUR - TWO DOWN AND TWO UP.

HOW CAN YOU
CURE SEASICKNESS?

BOLT DOWN
YOUR FOOD.

I'M GETTING SICK OF THESE JOKES!

WHERE DO COWS LIKE
TO GO FOR THEIR
HOLIDAYS?

MOO YORK.

HALF WAY

CLONK!!

WHAT DO YOU GET IF YOU CROSS THE ATLANTIC
WITH THE TITANIC? HALFWAY.

WHAT NEVER GETS ANY WETTER NO MATTER HOW MUCH IT RAINS ?

THE SEA.

WHEN I WENT TO AUSTRALIA I USED TO CHASE KANGAROOS ON HORSEBACK.

I DIDN'T KNOW KANGAROOS COULD RIDE HORSES.

NEITHER DID I !

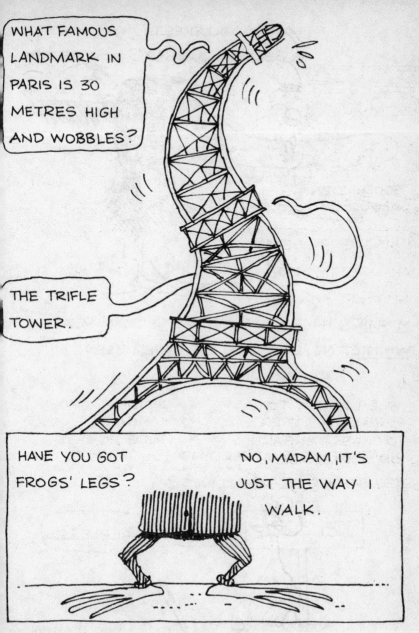

MOTORIST: DO YOU WANT A LIFT TO PARIS?

HITCHIKER: OUI, OUI.

MOTORIST: NOT IN MY CAR YOU DON'T!

175

HOW DO YOU GREET
A GERMAN BARBER?

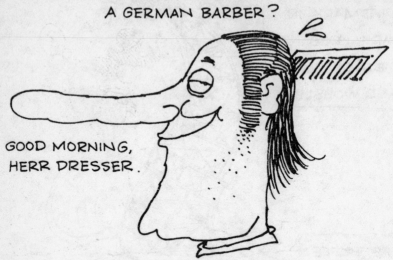

GOOD MORNING,
HERR DRESSER.

<u>MINNIE</u>: HAVE YOU EVER HAD GERMAN MEASLES?

<u>WINNIE</u>: NO, BUT THEN I'VE NEVER BEEN
TO GERMANY.

WHAT WOULD SWITZERLAND
BE WITHOUT ITS MOUNTAINS?

NOT THERE!

ALPLESS.

WHAT DO SPANISH FARMERS SAY TO THEIR HENS?

OLÉ!

WHICH ITALIAN SECRET SOCIETY BEATS PEOPLE UP WITH SHOPPING BASKETS?

THE RAFFIA.

WHAT'S THE DIFFERENCE BETWEEN A TUBE AND A DAFT DUTCHMAN?

ONE IS A HOLLOW CYLINDER; THE OTHER A SILLY HOLLANDER.

MRS. FEATHER: SO YOU'RE NOT GOING TO SPAIN THIS YEAR?

MRS. PITHER: NO, IT'S ITALY WE'RE NOT GOING TO. IT WAS SPAIN WE DIDN'T GO TO LAST YEAR.

SAMMY:
ARE YOU HUNGARY?
TAMMY:
YES, SIAM.
SAMMY:
COME IN AND I'LL FIJI.

WHEN IS A SHIP LIKE A FALL OF SNOW?

WHEN IT'S ADRIFT.

I DON'T UNDERSTAND

ROOMS WITH A SEA VIEW COST £5 EXTRA.

WHAT IF I PROMISE NOT TO LOOK?

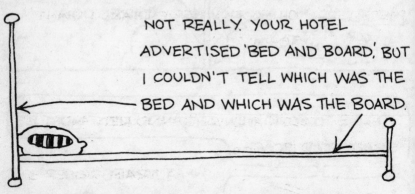

I HOPE YOU ENJOYED YOUR STAY, SIR.

NOT REALLY. YOUR HOTEL ADVERTISED 'BED AND BOARD,' BUT I COULDN'T TELL WHICH WAS THE BED AND WHICH WAS THE BOARD.

<u>HOTEL GUEST, ON PHONE</u>: IS THAT RECEPTION?

<u>RECEPTIONIST</u>: YES SIR. THIS IS THE FOURTH TIME YOU'VE RUNG. WHAT'S EATING YOU?

<u>HOTEL GUEST</u>: THAT'S WHAT I'D LIKE TO KNOW!

ME!

I'VE PUT ALL MY CLOTHES IN THAT LITTLE CUPBOARD WITH THE ROUND WINDOW.

OH DEAR, THAT'S THE PORTHOLE.

PASSENGER ON PLANE: DOES THIS PLANE FLY FASTER THAN THE SPEED OF SOUND?

STEWARDESS: NO MADAM.

PASSENGER: OH, GOOD. MY FRIEND AND I WANT TO TALK.

WHAT'S YELLOW AND WHITE AND RED AND TRAVELS AT 120 mph?

A TRAIN DRIVER'S EGG AND TOMATO SANDWICH.

HOW CAN YOU TELL WHEN A TRAIN HAS GONE?

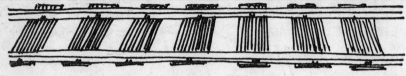

IT LEAVES TRACKS BEHIND.

WHY ISN'T IT SAFE TO GO TO BED ON A TRAIN?

BECAUSE TRAINS RUN OVER SLEEPERS.

POOP!
POOP!!
POOP!!!

WHAT'S THE HARDEST TRAIN TO CATCH?

THE 12.50, BECAUSE IT'S TEN TO ONE IF YOU CATCH IT.

DID YOU HEAR THERE WAS A FIGHT ON THE TRAIN?

WHAT HAPPENED?

THE INSPECTOR PUNCHED A TICKET.

WHOSE SKULL IS THAT?

AND WHOSE IS THE LITTLE SKULL BESIDE IT?

THAT'S THE SKULL OF THE EMPEROR NAPOLEON.

THAT'S THE SKULL OF THE EMPEROR NAPOLEON WHEN HE WAS A SMALL BOY.

183

184

PLEASE CALL ME A TAXI.

ALL RIGHT, SIR, YOU'RE A TAXI, BUT YOU LOOK MORE LIKE A ROLLS ROYCE TO ME.

OUR NEXT-DOOR NEIGHBOUR TRIED TO SWIM THE ENGLISH CHANNEL.

DID HE MAKE IT?

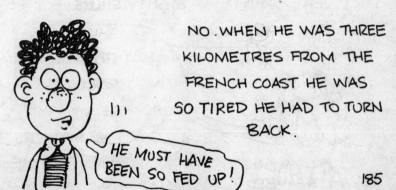

NO. WHEN HE WAS THREE KILOMETRES FROM THE FRENCH COAST HE WAS SO TIRED HE HAD TO TURN BACK.

HE MUST HAVE BEEN SO FED UP!

WHY ARE THE FINGERS ON THE STATUE OF
LIBERTY ELEVEN INCHES LONG?

BECAUSE IF THEY WERE TWELVE
INCHES LONG THEY WOULD BE A FOOT.

WHO SERVES THE
SPIRITS ON AN
AEROPLANE?

THE AIR
GHOSTESS.

DO YOU REALISE THAT YOU
WERE DRIVING AT EIGHTY MILES
PER HOUR?

BUT THAT'S
IMPOSSIBLE, I'VE
ONLY BEEN IN THE
CAR FIVE MINUTES.

POLICEMAN: DO YOU REALISE YOU WERE DRIVING AT TWENTY MILES AN HOUR OVER THE SPEED LIMIT?

CAR DRIVER: I'M SORRY, OFFICER, I WAS TRYING TO GET HOME BEFORE MY PETROL RAN OUT.

TWO BOYS MET AT A SKI RESORT. 'CAN I SHARE YOUR SKIS?' ASKED THE FIRST.
'OK,' REPLIED THE SECOND, 'WE'LL GO HALVES.'
'THANKS VERY MUCH,' SAID THE FIRST BOY.
'YES,' SAID THE SECOND, 'I'LL HAVE THEM GOING DOWNHILL AND YOU CAN HAVE THEM GOING UPHILL.'

WHAT'S THE CHEAPEST WAY TO GET TO AUSTRALIA?

BE BORN THERE.

DID YOU HEAR ABOUT THE SCOTSMAN WHO WASHED HIS KILT ?

HE COULDN'T DO A FLING WITH IT.

WHAT WAS THE WELSH COMEDIAN CALLED ?

DAI LAUGHING.

WHEN DOES AN IRISH POTATO CHANGE ITS NATIONALITY ?

WHEN IT BECOMES A FRENCH FRY.

TIM: WHAT'S HIGH, POINTED, AND HAS EARS?

TOM: I DON'T KNOW. WHAT?

TIM: A MOUNTAIN.

TOM: BUT WHAT ABOUT THE EARS?

TIM: HAVEN'T YOU EVER HEARD OF
MOUNTAINEERS?

A VISITOR WALKING IN THE SWISS ALPS LOOKED
WITH HORROR AT A STEEP SLOPE DOWN THE
MOUNTAIN AND SAID TO HIS GUIDE, 'YOU
SHOULD HAVE A SIGN THERE WARNING PEOPLE
OF DANGER.'

'WE USED TO HAVE,' REPLIED THE GUIDE.
'BUT NO ONE FELL DOWN THERE SO WE
REMOVED IT.'

A TOURIST IN A VILLAGE DEEP IN THE
COUNTRYSIDE ASKED A LOCAL WHERE THE
ROAD WENT TO.

'IT DOESN'T GO ANYWHERE,' REPLIED THE
MAN. 'IT STAYS RIGHT WHERE IT IS.'

DID YOU GO TO GREECE
FOR YOUR HOLIDAY?

I DON'T KNOW,
MY HUSBAND
BOUGHT THE
TICKETS.

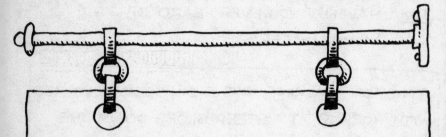

A TIRED AND HUNGRY TRAVELLER CAME TO AN INN CALLED THE GEORGE AND DRAGON, AND KNOCKED ON THE DOOR.

'COULD I HAVE SOMETHING TO EAT, PLEASE?' HE ASKED.

'NO,' SAID THE LANDLADY. 'WE'RE CLOSED.'

'WELL, COULD I HAVE A BED FOR THE NIGHT?'

'CERTAINLY NOT. GO AWAY.'

THE TRAVELLER WAITED A WHILE, AND THEN KNOCKED AGAIN. 'DO YOU THINK I COULD SPEAK TO GEORGE THIS TIME, PLEASE?'

ROOM 8

Old Sawbones

A ROOM FULL OF MEDICAL HISTORY

DOCTOR! DOCTOR! WILL THIS OINTMENT
CURE MY SPOTS?

I NEVER MAKE RASH PROMISES.

DOCTOR! DOCTOR! I KEEP THINKING I'M A
PAIR OF CURTAINS!

PULL YOURSELF TOGETHER, MAN.

DOCTOR! DOCTOR! I'VE ONLY GOT 59 SECONDS
TO LIVE!

SIT DOWN AND I'LL DEAL WITH YOU IN A
MINUTE.

DOCTOR! DOCTOR! I FEEL LIKE AN OLD SOCK!

WELL, I'LL BE DARNED!

DOCTOR! DOCTOR! I'VE
SWALLOWED A SPOON!

LIE DOWN AND DON'T
STIR.

DOCTOR! DOCTOR! I FEEL
LIKE A BELL!

GO HOME AND GIVE ME
A RING.

196

DOCTOR! DOCTOR!
I'VE GOT WATER ON
THE BRAIN!

TRY A TAP ON
THE HEAD.

HOT OR
COLD?

DOCTOR! DOCTOR!
I THINK I'M A DUSTBIN!

DON'T TALK
RUBBISH.

DOCTOR! DOCTOR!
I FEEL LIKE A CRICKET BALL.

HOWZAT!

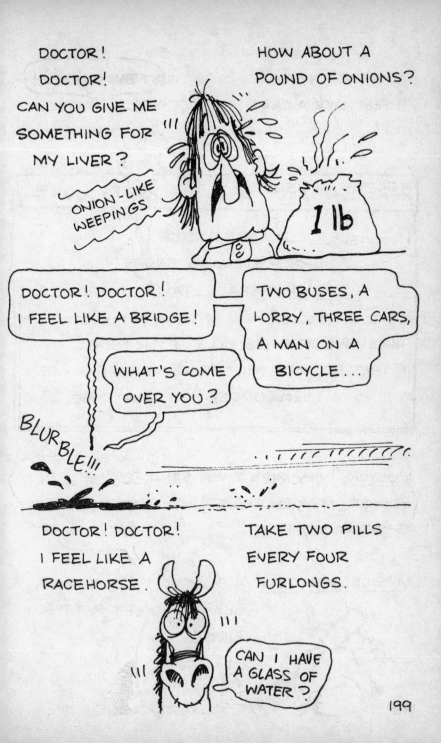

DOCTOR! DOCTOR!
I FEEL LIKE A CAR!

JUST PARK OVER
THERE A MINUTE,
WOULD YOU?

RARE EXAMPLE OF A NAUGHTY JOKE

DOCTOR! DOCTOR!
I KEEP STEALING THINGS.
WHAT SHALL I DO?

TAKE TWO OF THESE PILLS AFTER MEALS, AND
IF THAT DOESN'T HELP BRING ME BACK A VIDEO
RECORDER.

DOCTOR: WHY DIDN'T YOU SEND FOR ME
SOONER, MRS CRUMBLETUM? YOUR HUSBAND
IS SERIOUSLY ILL.

MRS CRUMBLETUM: I THOUGHT I'D GIVE HIM A
CHANCE TO GET BETTER
FIRST.

DOCTOR! DOCTOR!
I THINK I'M A GOAT.

HOW LONG HAVE YOU
THOUGHT SO?

EVER SINCE I
WAS A KID.

A KID IS
A BABY GOAT,
CHUMS!

DOCTOR! DOCTOR!
I FEEL LIKE A STRAWBERRY.

YOU ARE IN A JAM, AREN'T YOU?

DOCTOR! DOCTOR! WHAT CAN YOU GIVE ME
FOR FLAT FEET? HOW ABOUT A BICYCLE
PUMP?

203

IS IT SERIOUS, DOCTOR?

WELL, IF I WERE YOU I WOULDN'T
START READING ANY SERIALS.

MRS. FUMBLEFINGERS:
    Doctor, could you come and have a
    look at Grandma? She keeps saying
    she wants to die.

DOCTOR: You did the right thing by
        calling me.

DOCTOR: HOW IS THAT MEDICINE I PRESCRIBED
TO IMPROVE YOUR MEMORY WORKING?

PATIENT: WHAT MEDICINE?

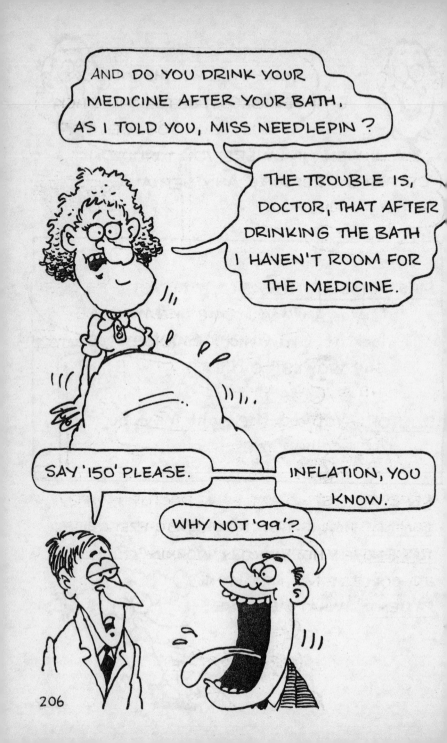

RECEPTIONIST: THAT NEW DOCTOR IS VERY FUNNY, HE'LL HAVE YOU IN STITCHES.

PATIENT: I HOPE NOT, I'VE ONLY COME IN TO COLLECT MY MEDICINE.

DOCTOR! DOCTOR! I FEEL LIKE A BIRD.

PERCH OVER THERE AND I'LL TWEET YOU IN A MOMENT.

DOCTOR! DOCTOR! I THINK I'M A FLY.
COME DOWN OFF THE CEILING AND WE'LL
TALK ABOUT IT.

I'M VERY NERVOUS, DOCTOR. I'VE NEVER HAD AN
OPERATION BEFORE.

I KNOW HOW YOU FEEL. I'VE
NEVER PERFORMED AN
OPERATION BEFORE.

209

DOCTOR:
GOOD MORNING, MRS VOLEVOICE, I HAVEN'T
SEEN YOU FOR AGES.

MRS VOLEVOICE:
NO, DOCTOR, I'VE BEEN ILL.

DOCTOR! DOCTOR! THE BABY'S SWALLOWED MY
PEN! WHAT SHALL I DO?
USE A PENCIL UNTIL I GET THERE.

PATIENT: DOCTOR, I'VE HAD STOMACH PAINS
EVER SINCE EATING SOME MUSSELS YESTERDAY.
DOCTOR: WERE THEY FRESH?
PATIENT: I DON'T KNOW.
DOCTOR: WELL, HOW DID THEY LOOK WHEN
YOU OPENED THEM UP?
PATIENT: *YOU MEAN YOU'RE SUPPOSED TO
OPEN THE SHELLS?*

DOCTOR! DOCTOR! I KEEP THINKING I'M A
DUMPLING.
        DON'T GET IN A STEW.

DOCTOR! DOCTOR! I KEEP THINKING I'M A CAT.
HOW LONG HAS THIS BEEN GOING ON?
EVER SINCE I HAD KITTENS.

MR LOONYBRAIN: I must tell you, doctor,
that I feel quite my old self again.
DOCTOR: In that case you need further
treatment.

DOCTOR:
IS YOUR COUGH BETTER THIS MORNING?
PATIENT:
IT SHOULD BE. I'VE BEEN PRACTISING ALL
NIGHT.

DOCTOR! DOCTOR! I CAN'T SLEEP, WHAT SHALL
I DO?
TRY LYING RIGHT ON THE EDGE OF THE BED.
YOU'LL SOON DROP OFF.

DOCTOR! DOCTOR! I FEEL LIKE A SNOOKER
BALL.
GET TO THE END OF THE QUEUE.

DOCTOR! DOCTOR!
I'VE SWALLOWED A
ROLL OF FILM.

LET'S HOPE
NOTHING
DEVELOPS.

PATIENT, WAKING AFTER OPERATION:

HOW AM I, NURSE?

NURSE:

WELL, THERE'S GOOD NEWS AND BAD NEWS.

PATIENT:

TELL ME THE BAD NEWS FIRST.

NURSE:

THE BAD NEWS IS, THE SURGEON SAWED OFF
BOTH YOUR FEET. THE GOOD NEWS IS THAT
THE MAN IN THE NEXT BED WANTS TO BUY
YOUR SLIPPERS.

MR TWILLITOE:

The doctor told me to take two of these pills on an empty stomach.

MR TURNIPTOE:

Did they do any good?

MR TWILLITOE:

I don't know, they kept rolling off in the night.

DOCTOR! DOCTOR! MY BROTHER THINKS HE'S A LIFT.

TELL HIM TO COME IN.

I CAN'T. HE DOESN'T STOP AT THIS FLOOR.

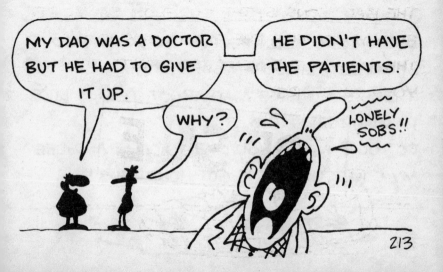

MY DAD WAS A DOCTOR BUT HE HAD TO GIVE IT UP.

WHY?

HE DIDN'T HAVE THE PATIENTS.

LONELY SOBS!!

'DOCTOR! DOCTOR! I THINK I'M A PUPPY.'

'SIT DOWN, PLEASE.'

I CAN'T, I'M NOT ALLOWED ON THE FURNITURE.

DOCTOR! DOCTOR! I THINK THERE ARE TWO OF ME.

I'LL SEE YOU ONE AT A TIME.

DOCTOR! DOCTOR! PEOPLE THINK I'M MAD BECAUSE I LIKE HAMBURGERS.
THERE'S NOTHING MAD ABOUT THAT. I LIKE HAMBURGERS TOO.
DO YOU? WOULD YOU LIKE TO COME AND SEE MY COLLECTION - I'VE GOT HUNDREDS!

C. 1910   C. 1827

ANYONE WHO GOES TO SEE A PSYCHIATRIST
WANTS HIS HEAD EXAMINING ...

DOCTOR: YOU MUST TAKE FOUR TEASPOONS
OF COUGH MIXTURE AFTER
EACH MEAL.
PATIENT: BUT WE'VE ONLY GOT THREE
TEASPOONS IN THE WHOLE HOUSE!

DOCTOR: YOU'VE HAD A BAD DOSE OF FLU.
TRY TO AVOID DRAUGHTS FOR A
WEEK OR SO.
PATIENT: CAN I PLAY CARDS INSTEAD?

A LITTLE GIRL BROKE HER WRIST. IT WAS
PUT INTO PLASTER, AND SHE ASKED,
'WHEN THE PLASTER'S TAKEN OFF, WILL
I BE ABLE TO PLAY THE PIANO?'
'OF COURSE,' REPLIED THE DOCTOR.
'THAT'S FUNNY,' SAID THE LITTLE GIRL.
'I COULDN'T BEFORE YOU PUT THE
PLASTER ON.'

YOU MUST TAKE ONE OF THESE PILLS FOUR TIMES A DAY.

HOW CAN I TAKE IT MORE THAN ONCE?

YEAH! HOW?

THICK DICK.

DOCTOR: AND DID YOU TRY COUNTING SHEEP TO HELP YOU FALL ASLEEP?

PATIENT: I DID. I COUNTED UP TO 637,439.

DOCTOR: AND DID YOU FALL ASLEEP?

PATIENT: NO, BY THEN IT WAS TIME TO GET UP!

217

WHO INVENTED ITALIAN RADIO?

MACARONI.

WHO CAN TELL ME
WHAT HCl STANDS FOR?

ER, IT'S ON THE TIP
OF MY TONGUE, MISS.

THEN YOU'D BETTER
SPIT IT OUT BECAUSE
IT'S HYDROCHLORIC
ACID!

---

*WATER.   **SULPHURIC ACID.

LITTLE BILLY'S DEAD,
WE'LL NEVER SEE HIM MORE,
'COS WHAT HE THOUGHT WAS H_2O*,
WAS H_2SO_4**.

WHAT HAPPENED WHEN THE WHEEL WAS INVENTED ?

IT CAUSED A REVOLUTION .

UGH ?

WHO CREATED THE LONDON UNDERGROUND ?

MOLES, SIR ?

THE SCIENCE TEACHER WAS TELLING THE CLASS ABOUT POLAR BEARS. 'IS IT TRUE THAT IF YOU CARRY A PIECE OF FISH IN YOUR POCKET A POLAR BEAR WON'T HURT YOU ?' ASKED JOHNNY.

BEFORE THE TEACHER COULD ANSWER, CLEVER CLARA PIPED UP, 'IT DEPENDS HOW FAST YOU CARRY IT !'

HOW CAN YOU MAKE A FIRE WITH TWO STICKS?

MAKE SURE ONE OF THEM IS A MATCH.

OLLIE: Which animals are best at maths?

MOLLY: Rabbits, because they multiply so well.

OLLIE: Rabbits may multiply well, but only a snake can be an adder.

NAME FOUR THINGS THAT CONTAIN MILK.

BUTTER, CHEESE AND TWO COWS.

HOMELESS 'N' REJECTED

WHAT KIND OF CREATURE IS A SLUG?

A HOMELESS SNAIL.

MOTHER: YOU CAME BOTTOM OUT OF TWENTY IN SCIENCE!

WILLIAM: IT COULD HAVE BEEN WORSE.

MOTHER: HOW?

WILLIAM: IF I'D BEEN IN TOM'S CLASS I'D HAVE COME BOTTOM OUT OF THIRTY.

WOULD YOU LIKE ME TO HELP YOU WITH YOUR SCIENCE HOMEWORK?

NO THANKS, DAD, I'D RATHER GET IT WRONG ON MY OWN.

SCIENCE TEACHER: WHO CAN TELL ME WHAT NITRATES ARE?

SALLY: THEY'RE CHEAPER THAN DAY RATES, MISS.

WHAT HAPPENED TO THE PLANT IN THE MATHS ROOM?

IT GREW SQUARE ROOTS.

WHAT'S THE COLDEST COUNTRY ON EARTH?

YES

CHILE.

CUTHBERT! YOU'VE BEEN DOING CAROL'S HOMEWORK AGAIN, HAVEN'T YOU? I RECOGNISED YOUR WRITING IN HER EXERCISE BOOK.

NO, MISS, I HAVEN'T, BUT WE DID USE THE SAME PEN.

DID YOU HEAR ABOUT THE BOY WHO CAME HOME FROM SCHOOL COVERED IN SPOTS? WHEN HIS MOTHER ASKED HIM WHAT WAS WRONG, HE REPLIED, 'I DON'T KNOW, BUT I THINK I'VE CAUGHT DECIMALS.'

ARE YOU GOOD AT SCIENCE?

WHAT DO YOU MEAN, YES AND NO?

WELL, YES AND NO.

YES, I'M NO GOOD AT SCIENCE.

$6 + 3 = 7$ $5 + 5 = 11$

WHEN DOES 5 AND 5 EQUAL 11?

$7 + 30 = 32$

$5 + 1 = 9$

WHEN YOU CAN'T ADD UP!

$177 + 236 = 414$

'BUT, MUM, I DON'T WANT TO GO TO SCHOOL, I REALLY DON'T.'

'DON'T BE SILLY, DEAR. YOU MUST GO. YOU'RE THE HEADMASTER!'

LETTIE: I'VE ADDED THESE SUMS UP TEN
TIMES, MISS.

MATHS TEACHER: WELL DONE.

LETTIE: AND HERE ARE MY TEN ANSWERS.

IF YOU HAD 37p IN ONE POCKET
AND 25p IN ANOTHER, WHAT WOULD
YOU HAVE?

TEACHER: CAN YOU ME SOMETHING THAT
CONDUCTS ELECTRICITY, SIMON?
SIMON: WHY, ER...
TEACHER: CORRECT.

WHAT HAPPENED
WHEN ELECTRICITY
WAS DISCOVERED?

SOMEONE GOT A
NASTY SHOCK.

SCIENCE TEACHER: WHO KNOWS WHAT A
LASER IS?
CHEEKY CHARLIE: IT'S WHAT CHINAMEN SHAVE
WITH.

WHAT'S A
POLYGON?

AN ESCAPED
PARROT.

WHERE
HAVE I ESCAPED
FROM?

WHAT'S POLYFILLA ?   PARROT FOOD.

ALBERT, A
FAT PARROT.

DID YOU HEAR WHAT HAPPENED WHEN SUSIE
FOUND A GRASS SNAKE ? SHE CALLED OUT,
'HERE'S A TAIL WITHOUT A BODY! '

WHAT'S THE MOST   NON-STICK GLUE.
   USELESS
INVENTION ?

WHAT DID THE MAD SCIENTIST SPEND YEARS
INVENTING ?

       A WATERPROOF TEABAG.

HOW WERE THE EXAM QUESTIONS ?

OK, BUT I HAD TROUBLE WITH THE ANSWERS.

FATHER : WHY DO YOU ALWAYS FAIL YOUR
SCIENCE EXAMS ?

DAVY : BECAUSE THEY ALWAYS SET THE
WRONG QUESTIONS.

WHAT DO YOU GET
IF YOU ADD 383 TO
245 AND THEN
SUBTRACT 317 ?

311 ?

THE WRONG ANSWER !

WHAT ARE THE SIGNS
OF IRON DEFICIENCY?

CRUMPLED
CLOTHES?

DID YOU KNOW THAT
MERCURY WAS AN
ANCIENT GOD WHO IS
NOW FOUND IN
THERMOMETERS?

I CAN'T SEE
ANYTHING!

TEACHER: NOW, CHILDREN, YOU UNDERSTAND
YOU CANNOT GET EGGS WITHOUT
CHICKENS.

BRIGHT BERTIE: MY GRANDAD DOES, MISS.
HE KEEPS GEESE.

WHY WAS THE WHEEL THE GREATEST INVENTION?

BECAUSE IT SET EVERYTHING ROLLING.

MATHS TEACHER: IF I HAD SIX ORANGES IN ONE HAND AND SEVEN IN THE OTHER, WHAT WOULD I HAVE?

SUSIE: GIANT HANDS, MISS!

THE CHEMISTRY TEACHER WAS SHOWING THE CLASS HOW ACID COULD DISSOLVE METALS, AND DROPPED A £1 COIN IN A BEAKERFUL. 'DO YOU THINK THE ACID WILL DISSOLVE IT?' HE ASKED.

'NO, SIR,' REPLIED THE BOY.

'RIGHT, BUT HOW DID YOU KNOW?' ASKED THE TEACHER.

'BECAUSE YOU WOULDN'T HAVE DROPPED IT IN IF IT WAS GOING TO DISSOLVE!'

P.E. TEACHER: GRAHAM, YOU ARE HOPELESS AT
GAMES. HAVE YOU EVER COME
FIRST IN ANYTHING?

GILBERT: HE'S FIRST IN THE DINNER QUEUE
EVERY DAY, MISS.

WHAT'S THE LONGEST NIGHT OF THE YEAR?

A FORTNIGHT.

I THOUGHT A FORTNIGHT WAS TWO WEEKS!!?

THIS COMPUTER WILL DO HALF YOUR WORK FOR YOU.

WONDERFUL! I'LL TAKE TWO!

WHAT TRAVELS FASTER, HEAT OR COLD?
HEAT, YOU CAN CATCH COLD.

CAN YOU TYPE? NOT VERY WELL. BUT I CAN RUB OUT AT 50 WORDS A MINUTE.

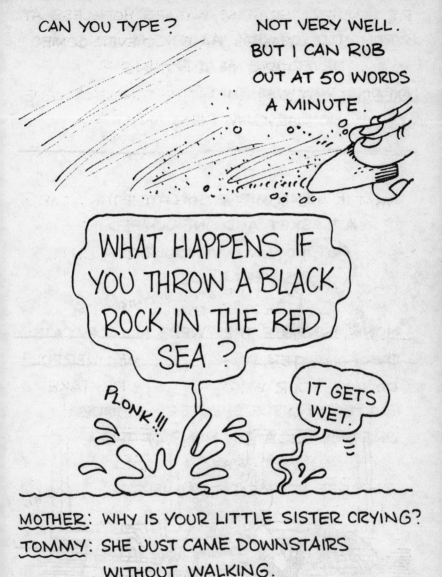

WHAT HAPPENS IF YOU THROW A BLACK ROCK IN THE RED SEA?

PLONK!!!

IT GETS WET.

MOTHER: WHY IS YOUR LITTLE SISTER CRYING?
TOMMY: SHE JUST CAME DOWNSTAIRS WITHOUT WALKING.

WHAT CAN YOU HOLD WITHOUT YOUR HANDS?
YOUR BREATH.

BYRON: DID YOU HEAR ABOUT THE LIONS WHO
NEVER ATE MEAT ?
MYRON: WHY WAS THAT ?
BYRON: NO ONE GAVE THEM ANY.

IF THERE WERE SIX CATS IN
A BASKET AND ONE JUMPED
OUT, HOW MANY WOULD
BE LEFT ?

NONE, BECAUSE THEY WERE ALL COPY CATS.

TEN PEOPLE WERE SHELTERING UNDER
ONE UMBRELLA BUT NONE OF THEM
GOT WET. WHY ?
BECAUSE IT WASN'T RAINING.

SO WHY WERE
THEY UNDER
THE
UMBRELLA?

WHAT WOULD YOU
DO WITH A WOMBAT?

PLAY WOM, OF
COURSE!

WOM!

TEACHER: WHO CAN TELL ME WHAT JOHN
LOGIE BAIRD WAS FAMOUS FOR?

PADDY: HIS MEMORY.

TEACHER: WHY DO YOU SAY THAT?

PADDY: BECAUSE THERE'S A STATUE
ERECTED TO IT.

WHO SETTLED IN
THE WEST BEFORE
ANYONE ELSE?

THE SUN.

FED-UP
YEE HAR!

A MAN WENT TO A SPACE
STATION AND ASKED FOR
A TICKET TO THE MOON.

'SORRY, SIR,' SAID THE
ATTENDANT. 'THE MOON'S
FULL RIGHT NOW.'

WHICH IS HEAVIER, A
FULL MOON OR A
HALF MOON?

A HALF MOON, BECAUSE
A FULL MOON IS LIGHTER.

BLONK!!

THAT STAR THERE IS
MARS.

WHICH IS PA'S,
THEN?

TEACHER:
WHAT ARE YOU DRAWING?

MAISIE:
A PICTURE OF HEAVEN.

TEACHER:
BUT NO ONE KNOWS WHAT HEAVEN LOOKS
LIKE.

MAISIE:
THEY WILL WHEN I'VE FINISHED, WON'T THEY?

THE TEACHER TOLD EVERYONE WHO WANTED
TO GO TO HEAVEN TO PUT UP THEIR HAND.
THE ONLY CHILD THAT DIDN'T WAS YOUNG
EDWARD. 'DON'T YOU WANT TO GO TO
HEAVEN, EDWARD? ASKED THE TEACHER.
'OH, YES, MISS,' HE REPLIED. 'BUT MY MUM
SAID I SHOULD GO STRAIGHT HOME AFTER
SCHOOL.'

‹HEAVEN   HOME›

WHY DID THE SCIENTIST TAKE A RULER TO BED?
SO HE COULD SEE HOW LONG HE SLEPT.

WHAT'S THE EASIEST WAY TO BE A
SCIENTIST IN SOUTH AMERICA ?

BE BORN THERE!

OLD REFRIGERATORS
NEVER DIE, THEY JUST
LOSE THEIR COOL.

'YOU'VE GOT YOUR HAT ON BACK TO FRONT.'
'HOW DO YOU WHICH WAY I'M GOING?'

`DID YOU TRY SURF-RIDING IN
CALIFORNIA ?'
'I TRIED TO, BUT I COULDN'T GET THE
HORSE NEAR THE WATER.'

CHEER UP, MR WOBBLECHIN,
WE'VE CURED YOU.

I KNOW. BUT WOULDN'T
YOU BE SAD IF YOU'D
THOUGHT YOU WERE
NAPOLEON ALL YOUR
LIFE AND THEN FOUND
OUT YOU WERE NOBODY?

NOT NAPOLEON !

WHICH SCIENTIST HAS THE BIGGEST HEAD ?

THE ONE WITH THE BIGGEST HAT !

IF YOUR NOSE RUNS AND YOUR FEET SMELL, WHAT'S THE MATTER WITH YOU?

YOU'VE BEEN MADE UPSIDE-DOWN.

WHAT'S THE SMALLEST ROOM IN THE WORLD?

A MUSHROOM.

DAVE: WHICH MONTH HAS 28 DAYS ?
MAVE: THEY ALL HAVE !

WHAT'S THE EASIEST
WAY TO GET CLOSE TO
MONEY ?

STAND BY THE
CASH
DISPENSER IN THE
BANK WALL.

FIRST SCIENTIST: DID YOU MEET YOUR
DAUGHTER AT THE AIRPORT ?
SECOND SCIENTIST: OH, NO, I'VE KNOWN HER
FOR YEARS !

'HOW'S YOUR DAD GETTING ON IN HOSPITAL ?'
'HE'S TAKEN A TURN FOR THE NURSE.'

PATIENT IN HOSPITAL: DOES YOUR WIFE MISS YOU?
SECOND PATIENT: NOT OFTEN, SHE'S A VERY
GOOD SHOT. THAT'S WHY I'M HERE.

ROOM 10

Old Chestnuts

KNOCK, KNOCK.
WHO'S THERE?
LETTUCE.
LETTUCE WHO?
LETTUCE IN, PLEASE, IT'S RAINING.

QUIET PLEASE.

KNOCK, KNOCK.
WHO'S THERE?
FELIX.
FELIX WHO?
FELIX MY ICE-CREAM AGAIN I'LL BASH HIM.

KNOCK, KNOCK.
WHO'S THERE?
SNOW.
SNOW WHO?
SNOW USE, I CAN'T REMEMBER MY NAME.

WHAT DID THE MAYONNAISE SAY TO THE
FRIDGE? 'CLOSE THE DOOR, I'M DRESSING.'

KNOCK, KNOCK JOKES

WHAT DID THE TIE SAY TO THE HAT?

'YOU GO ON AHEAD AND I'LL HANG AROUND.'

WHAT DO REINDEER SAY BEFORE THEY TELL YOU A JOKE?

'THIS ONE WILL SLEIGH YOU!'

WHERE CAN YOU ALWAYS FIND DIAMONDS? IN A PACK OF CARDS.

WHAT HAS ONE HORN AND GIVES MILK? A MILK FLOAT.

WHAT DO YOU CALL A CAT WHO SWALLOWED A DUCK? A DUCK-FILLED FATTY PUSS.

WHAT DO YOU CALL A MAN WITH A PAPER BAG ON HIS HEAD? RUSSELL.

WHAT DO YOU CALL A MAN WITH A SEAGULL ON HIS HEAD? CLIFF.

WHAT DO YOU CALL A MAN WITH A CAR ON HIS HEAD? JACK.

JOHN: HAVE YOU EVER SEEN A DOG MAKE A RABBIT HUTCH?

CON: NO, BUT I'VE SEEN A FOX MAKE A CHICKEN RUN.

WHAT'S A COMPLETE WASTE OF TIME? TELLING A HAIR-RAISING STORY TO A BALD MAN!

WHAT'S GREY, HAS FOUR LEGS AND A TRUNK? A MOUSE GOING ON HOLIDAY

WHAT GETS WETTER AS IT DRIES?

A TOWEL.

WHEN DOES A HORSE HAVE SIX LEGS? WHEN IT HAS A RIDER ON ITS BACK.

WHAT WOULD HAPPEN IF PIGS COULD FLY?

BACON WOULD GO UP.

AIRBORNE OIKINGS?

TRAVELLING ON A TRAIN, A WOMAN WAS GETTING IRRITATED BY A GIRL NEXT TO HER WHO KEPT SNIFFING. 'HAVEN'T YOU GOT A HANDKERCHIEF?' SHE DEMANDED CROSSLY.

'YES,' SAID THE GIRL. 'BUT MY MUM WOULDN'T LIKE ME TO LEND IT TO A STRANGER.'

WHAT DO YOU DO WITH A GREEN MONSTER?

WAIT UNTIL IT'S RIPE.

WHAT DO YOU DO WITH A BLUE MONSTER?

TRY TO CHEER IT UP.

LADY IN CLOTHES SHOP: MAY I TRY ON THAT RED DRESS IN THE WINDOW?

SHOP ASSISTANT: NO, MADAM, YOU'LL HAVE TO USE THE CHANGING-ROOM LIKE EVERYONE ELSE.

DID YOU HEAR THE STORY OF THE THREE WELLS? NO? WELL, WELL, WELL.

OLDEST JOKE

DID YOU HEAR THE
STORY OF THE THREE
EGGS?
NO? TOO BAD.

TEACHER: AND WHAT MIGHT YOUR NAME BE,
YOUNG MAN?
NEW BOY: IT MIGHT BE CLARENCE, BUT IT ISN'T,
HE'S MY COUSIN.

A MAN FOUND A PARCEL OF KIPPERS ON A BUS
AND TOOK THEM TO THE LOST PROPERTY OFFICE.
THE ATTENDANT TOOK DOWN THE DETAILS, AND
THEN SAID, 'COME BACK IN SIX MONTHS. IF NO ONE'S
CLAIMED THEM BY THEN, THEY'RE YOURS.'

WHAT TIME IS IT
WHEN THE CLOCK
STRIKES THIRTEEN?
TIME TO GET A NEW
CLOCK.

WHAT HAS A
BOTTOM AT THE
TOP?
A LEG.

248

WHAT WALKS AROUND ON ITS HEAD ALL DAY?
A NAIL IN YOUR SHOE.

WHEN SHOULD YOU FEED HIPPOPOTAMUS MILK TO A BABY? WHEN IT'S A BABY HIPPOPOTAMUS.

WHAT GOES 'OOM, OOM'? A COW WALKING BACKWARDS.

TEACHER: WHAT CAME AFTER THE STONE AGE
AND THE IRON AGE?
SAMANTHA: THE SAUS-AGE?

TEACHER: WHAT DOES IT MEAN WHEN THE
BAROMETER FALLS?
CHRISSIE: UM, THAT THE NAIL HAS COME OUT
OF THE WALL?

TEACHER: WHEN WAS THE FORTH BRIDGE
BUILT?
MANDY: AFTER THE THIRD ONE HAD
FALLEN DOWN.

VICAR: DO YOU SAY A PRAYER BEFORE DINNER?

VICKY: NO, THERE'S NO NEED. MY MUM'S A VERY GOOD COOK.

POMPOUS OLD MAN: ONE OF MY RELATIVES DIED AT WATERLOO.

MILLY: REALLY! WHICH PLATFORM?

DAD: NOW STOP FIGHTING, CHARLIE! YOU MUST LEARN TO GIVE AND TAKE.

CHARLIE: I DID. I GAVE CLAUD A BLACK EYE AND TOOK HIS APPLE.

WHAT DO YOU GET IF YOU EAT CHRISTMAS DECORATIONS? TINSELITIS.

WHAT'S BLACK AND WHITE AND GOES AROUND ON EIGHT WHEELS? A NUN ON ROLLER SKATES.

COCKNEY TEACHER: WHAT'S THE DIFFERENCE BETWEEN A BUFFALO AND A BISON?

COCKNEY PUPIL: YOU CAN'T WASH YOUR HANDS IN A BUFFALO.

WHY DID THE APPLE
GO OUT WITH THE PRUNE?
BECAUSE HE COULDN'T
FIND A DATE.

WHAT DO ESKIMOS
CALL THEIR MONEY?
ICED LOLLY.

TEACHER: IF YOU FOUND SOME MONEY, WOULD
YOU KEEP IT?

JENNY: OH NO.

TEACHER: GOOD GIRL. WHAT WOULD YOU DO
WITH IT?

JENNY: I'D SPEND IT.

'HAS YOUR BROTHER GOT A HOBBY HE CAN
STICK TO?' 'YES, HE SPENDS HIS TIME GLUED
TO THE TELEVISION.'

CUSTOMER: DO YOU SELL INVISIBLE INK?

SHOP ASSISTANT: YES, WHAT COLOUR WOULD
YOU LIKE?

WHAT GOES 99-PLONK, 99-PLONK?

A CENTIPEDE WITH A WOODEN LEG.

WHAT TIME IS IT WHEN YOU GO TO THE
DENTIST? TOOTH-HURTY.

NATURE WARDEN: YOU CAN'T CATCH FISH
WITHOUT A PERMIT.
HARRY: I'M DOING QUITE WELL WITH WORMS,
THANK YOU.

WHAT'S VERY LARGE, GREY AND MUTTERS?
A MUMBO-JUMBO.

LIBRARIAN: DO YOU LIKE KIPLING?
READER: I DON'T KNOW, I'VE NEVER KIPPLED.

'DOCTOR, DOCTOR, I'VE GOT CARROTS GROWING OUT OF MY EARS!'
'GOOD HEAVENS! HOW DID THAT HAPPEN?'
'I DON'T KNOW, I PLANTED TOMATOES.'

WHERE IS EVERYONE BEAUTIFUL?
IN THE DARK.

LEN: DID YOU HEAR THE STORY OF THE DIRTY SHIRT?
KEN: NO.
LEN: THAT'S ONE ON YOU.

CUSTOMER: TWO LAMB CHOPS PLEASE. AND MAKE THEM LEAN.
BUTCHER: CERTAINLY, MADAM, WHICH WAY?

DID YOU HEAR ABOUT THE WOMAN WHO WENT ON A BANANA AND COCONUT DIET? SHE DIDN'T LOSE ANY WEIGHT BUT SHE COULDN'T HALF CLIMB TREES!